LOSSES & CHANGES

Bell, Carolyn Ann

RECOVERY
DISCOVERY

LOSSES & CHANGES

Finding Hope in Life's Difficult Times

Randy Reynolds & David Lynn

ZondervanPublishingHouse
Grand Rapids, Michigan
A Division of HarperCollins*Publishers*

Losses and Changes

Requests for information should be addressed to:
Zondervan Publishing House
Grand Rapids, Michigan 49530

ISBN 0-310-57301-7

Edited by Linda Vanderzalm
Interior design by Ann Cherryman
Cover design by Lecy Design
Cover photo by Dan Hummel

Printed in the United States of America

92 93 94 95 96 97 / DP / 10 9 8 7 6 5 4 3 2 1

1. Cut Loose and in Pain

RECOVERY FOCUS

- Examine the types of losses and changes people experience.
- Identify the losses and changes you have experienced.
- Learn how people respond to loss and change through grief.

RECOVERY INFORMATION

Everything in life is fragile. That reality comes crashing on you when you lose something or someone important or when things unexpectedly change. It hurts deeply when you lose things you have counted on. You feel cheated, that life wasn't supposed to be this way. You get angry, become confused, and feel disoriented.

Change and loss are as much a part of life as day and night. But even though they are common, they still cause difficulty and pain. You are probably reading this book because of pain in your life. You may be feeling no one understands the struggles you're having with your changes or losses. You may want some practical things to do to help deal with your pain and learn how to move on through your loss. We pray this book will help you deal with many aspects of loss and changes so that you can move toward recovery.

CHANGES AND LOSSES

It has been said that the only constant in life is change. The writer of the letter to the Hebrews talks about the fact that all "created things" can be shaken or don't last. Only God is constant and dependable.

Whether your losses are minor, like misplaced keys, or major, like a loved one lost to death, the pain in your loss is proportionate to the amount of investment you have in what you lose. That is different for each person. What would be a difficult change for some will not be for others. One woman said, "I did okay when I found out my sister had cancer, and I took my husband's job transfer well, but when my cat was killed under the garage door I couldn't stop crying." A man said, "I felt guilty that I was so devastated at the loss of my job. I have a great family, enough money, and other things I can do, but it seemed like the end of the world when, after twenty years as an engineer, I was laid off. I've been so depressed and can't seem to get going again."

Loss and change often cause pain because you feel as if your security has been removed. You may no longer feel connected to what was supplying you with life. Your life has been shaken, and you feel lost, disoriented, devastated, and alone in your grief.

Your expectation that life shouldn't be like this may cause you to struggle more with the process of letting go and moving on in life. If you feel that life owes you things or that your loss or change shouldn't have happened to you, you may have an overwhelming sense that life is unfair.

It's normal to feel angry during times of change or loss; resistance to change is human. However, in order to recover from grief and loss, you must be willing to let go of the expectations that don't match your experience.

CHANGES

Many changes come into your life: a job change, a move to another home, a marriage, having a child, a child starting school, a change in income, a lifestyle change, a need to change direction or purpose after achieving a goal, moving from adolescence to adulthood or from adulthood to midlife, having a change from good health to new limitations. Transitions take their toll—even when they are planned.

1. What changes affect your life right now? List them.

2. What job or career changes are you going through?

3. What relationship changes are you going through? What has changed?

4. What changes in values, beliefs, or purposes are you involved in?

LOSSES

Changes are often positive as well as negative, but losses are usually experienced as negative. The loss of something external often triggers the loss of many internal things. The loss of someone you love may cause you to feel hopeless, insecure, apathetic, and worthless: you've lost something external—the person—but you've also lost something internal—your hope, confidence, motivation, and esteem. A part of you dies when you lose someone or something close to you.

Losses can be abstract, such as the loss of a dream, longing, ideal, goal, belief, expectation, or perception. Losses can be concrete, such as the loss of a leg, a friend, a church community, a relative, a home, a job, or a marriage. Nothing cuts more deeply than a loss. If you "collect losses" and don't work through them or recover from them, you will experience a damaging cumulative reaction to the losses.

1. What losses are you struggling with? List them.

2. Which are the most painful?

3. Which losses do you have a difficult time talking about without feeling overwhelmed?

4. What other losses might be affecting you? List them.

GRIEF

Change and loss produce grief. Although grief is a normal part of life, it can be excruciatingly painful. Grief can be described as acute emotional suffering. Grief hurts, and that pain may come out in sobs of sadness, angry fits, or overwhelming feelings of guilt or shame. The good news is the pain will leave. It will not always hurt this deeply. But recovering from grief takes time.

In many cultures grieving is a part of rites of passage. Mothers grieve with older women when their boys become men. Grievers are available to help release the emotion that accompanies loss, to help people heal and move on in their lives. Everyone in the village mourns a death; grief, in these cultures, is a communal experience that brings a comfort, connection, and nurture.

In our culture, grief often brings alienation and loneliness. We isolate to protect ourselves from having more pain or disappointment. However, we then may not get the nurture we need to help us in the recovery process. It often helps to hear that others are having similar experiences and that we aren't the only ones in pain. A woman who had had three miscarriages was struggling over the disappointment of being unable to give birth. She found herself feeling angry at mothers with young children. She was ashamed of these feelings and avoided people because of this angry reaction. She attended a grief group and heard a mother who had lost a child share very similar feelings. She felt relief and was able to break out of her isolation.

People in grief may quit caring for themselves in the most basic areas. Often the emotional pain is so great that they don't feel like eating. A college student who suffered a broken engagement lost twenty-five pounds in six weeks from not eating. Another college student gained fifty pounds in six months trying to comfort himself through a difficult loss.

The emotional fixation on pain brings many people to a restless state in which they can't sleep. Others stop exercising because of their grief and feel worse. Although these responses are understandable, they are not healthy. In order to bring some stability to your grief process, you must take care of your needs for eating right, getting enough sleep, and exercising.

Depression is a normal part of grief and so are thoughts of escape. However, if you are suicidal, you must talk with someone who can help you. If you can't stabilize your sleeping or eating, get help from your doctor. Contact a hotline, hospital, or a counselor for further help. There is someone who cares about you in your pain.

BEGIN TO GRIEVE

Recognizing that your grief is a normal part of your losses and changes may help you begin to express and work through it. Consider these practical ways of recognizing and expressing your grief.

Find a safe place, person, or group and begin to release your feelings. Releasing your feelings may leave you drained, but you may experience peace or rest as you give yourself the freedom to express the thoughts and feelings you wrestle with inside.

You may want to arrange a time to grieve. This may sound a bit strange, but if you give yourself twenty minutes in the morning, for example, you can count on that time to uncork your feelings. If intense feelings pop up at other times of the day, express them then if you can. Or if your feelings come at a time and place that are not appropriate for you to grieve, you may find strength in knowing that you can hold the feelings until your "grief appointment" the next morning.

Start a journal in which you express your feelings and insights. The daily discipline of writing out your feelings may be an important step in your recovery. One of the benefits of a journal is that after several weeks or months of keeping it, you can reread what you have written and see your growth. Marian kept a journal after her husband, Jonathan, had died. She felt the journal became an important device in recording her feelings. Marian had found it very hard to talk about her feelings to other people. It's not that she didn't want to admit the feelings or move beyond them, but she felt to give them up would somehow betray Jonathan, and she would forget her feelings toward him. She was confused. In keeping a journal, she could "keep" her feelings while she gave them up.

Take care of yourself during your grief. Give yourself the freedom to rest more and be distant from some of the demands in your life. Take care of yourself physically, emotionally, and spiritually.

RECOVERY PROBERS

1. How do you deal with grief in your life?

2. How did your childhood family deal with grief?

3. Do you feel that grief is an indication that you aren't trusting God? Explain your response.

4. Do people put pressure on you to be done with your grief? How?

5. Where and with whom do you let your feelings out?

6. What practical things do you do to feel better?

RECOVERY GUIDE

The Bible makes it clear that we all will have losses and changes in this life. This is to be expected and it will bring grief and pain. The most godly people of both the New and Old Testaments had many grief experiences.

Read Ecclesiastes 3:1–2, 4.

1. **The New American Standard translation says there is "an appointed time for everything," as if God allows or delegates seasons in our lives. In what ways is your struggle a result of your expectation that life shouldn't be the way it is?**

2. **How does this Scripture passage show you another reality?**

3. **Is it okay to grieve according to this passage?**

Read John 16:33.

1. **What does Jesus promise we will have in him?**

2. **What does Jesus say we will have in the world?**

3. **Is this something you have dealt with before? How?**

Read John 11:35.

1. **Some people feel that if we have enough faith in God, we will not grieve. But the Scripture says the opposite. When Lazarus died and Jesus came to raise him from the dead and saw Mary weeping, Jesus wept. Why did Jesus weep if he knew that Lazarus would shortly be raised from the dead?**

2. **Did Jesus lack faith because he hurt and wept with Mary? How does this comfort you?**

Read Lamentations 3:1–3, 16–18.

1. **Jeremiah, an Old Testament prophet, went through all the feelings of grief as Israel was taken into captivity and suffered loss. What feelings does Jeremiah express in this passage?**

2. **What similar feelings do you have?**

RECOVERY GOALS

The goal of this chapter is to help you begin to see your grief as a normal part of loss and change in your life and allow yourself room to grieve. For some people the feelings of grief are so intense that they are afraid to let them out for fear they will lose control.

1. What safe place will you choose to release your feelings?

2. What trusted person can help you cope with your grief?

3. In what ways would a "grief appointment" be helpful for you? When will you set up these "appointments"?

4. Will keeping a journal be helpful for you? When will you start?

5. What will you do to take care of yourself physically?

6. What will you do to take care of yourself emotionally?

7. What will you do to take care of yourself spiritually?

2. Stability

RECOVERY FOCUS

- Gain stability.
- Give yourself permission to grieve and time to recover.
- Take care of yourself in healthy ways.

RECOVERY INFORMATION

Your grief may make you feel terrible. You hear a song on the radio, see a picture, or smell a fragrance and feel overwhelmed with sadness. You may receive a bill or realize you could have done something differently or have to do a job as the result of the change and feel very angry at yourself or others. You are tired of being controlled by these feelings and want some emotional stability. Just about the time you begin to feel normal, something else triggers your grief and off you go again, hoping no one notices.

What can you do to feel better and not have so many emotional ups and downs? First, give yourself time for the emotional roller coaster to begin to level out. Then, consider the following practical ways of gaining some stability.

GETTING YOUR FEET BACK UNDER YOU

Research shows that if you are able to be nurturing to yourself during times of loss, change, or stress, you will do much better in recovery. The grief process is different for different people in that the time of grieving varies with different people. Major losses or changes take a couple of years to work through for most people. However, finding nurture in the process helps stabilize your emotions.

Josh and Kathy had been knocked off their feet when their son drowned in a neighbor's swimming pool. They both were hard workers and tried to keep up with their work even through this deep grief. They found themselves, however, pulling inside themselves with a heartache that would not go away.

After a couple of months of struggling alone, they started

attending a grief-recovery group at a local church. They found others with deep losses. One man had lost his wife after she had been in a coma for two years. A woman had lost her mother to cancer, and a man had lost his business and his parents in the same year. Josh and Kathy found love and acceptance of their feelings through this group. The members of the group truly understood their grief and prayed for them on a weekly basis.

Both Josh and Kathy began to feel better and began to do more nurturing things for themselves and each other. Their "I-don't-care-anymore" attitude was subsiding. They also began to look forward to little things, which at first didn't make them feel much better because the ache hurt too much. "Nothing makes me feel good," Kathy would say. Eventually, both of them began to enjoy little pleasures and would talk about them with each other. Also, hearing others' pain and grief didn't depress them as they thought it would; rather, it helped them not feel so alone.

Josh and Kathy were also able to grieve more freely because of their experience in the group. Kathy had felt Josh didn't care at times because he didn't show his grief as much as she did. The truth was that Josh felt he had to be strong for Kathy and was trying to cover his feelings, which distanced him from her. As he was able to grieve more freely, Kathy was relieved and felt closer to Josh. Going to the group was a way that Josh and Kathy found nurture for their wounds of loss. The group was a safe place for them, a place where they could share their deepest thoughts and feelings and feel protected and loved.

What are you doing to get some nurture to help you with your recovery? Everyone grieves a little differently. While some things minister to other people, they may not minister to you. Read the following checklist and check those things you enjoy and can do to gain recovery.

- ☐ Eat well
- ☐ Draw closer to God
- ☐ Exercise regularly
- ☐ Minimize decision making
- ☐ Get enough rest and sleep
- ☐ Express feelings of grief
- ☐ Find someone to laugh with
- ☐ Spend time with people that you enjoy
- ☐ Pamper self, like buying something new

- ☐ Do something you enjoy every day
- ☐ Pray
- ☐ Take a trip
- ☐ Go to a movie
- ☐ Lie in the sun
- ☐ Read the Bible
- ☐ Watch a sunset
- ☐ Read a good book
- ☐ Take a hot bath
- ☐ Go out for ice cream
- ☐ Go to a peaceful place
- ☐ Listen to some good music
- ☐ Take a walk in a beautiful place

HEALTHY VS. UNHEALTHY CARE

Going through change and loss will affect your values and your self-concept. What was important before may no longer be important to you.

Ben, who had lived to work his way up in the company, is without a job. He feels as if his life has no purpose. He knows in his head that God values him and has a purpose for him. However, these realities are hard for him to grasp in his grief. If he does well through the grief process, he will find his self-esteem is flexible to change. Ben said, "I feel as if I have failed. Now that I'm not able to support my family, I feel worthless."

If your self-esteem is resting on thin ice, you may begin to sink when you experience a loss or change. Your loss will expose the source of your self-esteem and security. The loss may help you see that you are more than your job, home, hobbies, achievements, relationships, or whatever your identity was invested in. You can survive losses and failures and with God's help find new life.

However, some people make wrong turns during grief because they feel that nothing matters, not even themselves. Jeff went through a divorce and turned back to alcohol to relieve his pain. This really increased his pain in the long run.

Be aware that denying the pain of your grief may tempt you into unhealthy behaviors that can destroy more of your life. A young man who didn't have very much support had put most of his time into a girlfriend. When she broke off their relationship, he began stealing money from his mother's purse to be able to go out and distract himself from his pain.

It's normal to regress some during times of grief, to go back to some childish or adolescent behaviors. Allow yourself some grace here, but be careful not to head in a downward spiral. Jim, during a midlife crisis, felt like a failure because his dreams weren't being realized. He began blaming his wife for his personal sense of failure. This ended in a divorce, which increased his pain even more. He had begun to cope with his loss by becoming more isolated from his family and venting angry feelings when he was around them. He had a difficult time verbalizing and taking responsibility for his feelings of loss and failure. His life was on the way to disaster. Only after Jim was able to face his pain and grief over his unfulfilled dreams did he begin to make progress.

It's tempting to gain comfort during times of loss by using coping mechanisms that give short-term relief but don't resolve our grief. Read the following checklist and check the coping mechanisms you use in dealing with your grief.

- ☐ Overeating
- ☐ Using drugs
- ☐ Drinking alcohol
- ☐ Blaming others and distancing
- ☐ Escaping in sexual relationships or fantasies
- ☐ Quitting life tasks and isolating
- ☐ Breaking off stable relationships
- ☐ Overspending or ignoring your budget
- ☐ Escaping in ways that hinder your ability to function
- ☐ Venting anger toward authority figures and breaking rules

If you are using these things to help you through your grief, we recommend that you see someone who can help you. You may talk to a doctor or therapist about the depression side of your grief. You may also need to find an environment that can provide you some stability.

Everyone has some regression during times of grief, but regression is there to help you feel good and safe, not to put you in more pain and loss. As you begin to let go, you will find the pain will begin to diminish and that new life will come. It's important that you move to things that help you stabilize during this grief process and don't cause more losses.

RECOVERY PROBERS

1. What are you doing to help you stabilize in your grief?

2. Do you give yourself permission to express your angry feelings in your losses and changes? How?

3. Do you give yourself permission to express your sad feelings in your losses and changes? How?

4. How do your losses make you feel out of control and afraid?

5. Does God help you deal with your grief or does thinking about him make you more upset? Explain.

6. What responses to your pain may be unhealthy and cause you or others more pain?

7. In what ways might you be denying your pain and then pushing others away or being hurtful because of it?

RECOVERY GUIDE

Read 2 Corinthians 1:3–4.

1. In what areas do you need comfort?

2. In what ways has God been the "God of all comfort" to you?

3. How are you receiving God's comfort?

4. What other people have been a comfort to you?

Read Hebrews 12:15.

1. Part of receiving comfort and grace is being able to receive small pleasures in your life and to view them as gifts from God's hand. How can you miss God's grace?

2. How does God's grace soften your heart?

Read Lamentations 3:22–25.

1. Part of finding comfort is seeking God and his presence, like the small child who runs to the loving arms of a concerned parent after getting hurt. How are you seeking God?

2. What does it mean to you when the Scripture says, "The Lord is my portion"?

3. How is God's compassion "new every morning" for you?

4. What does it mean in your life right now to "wait" on God and find your hope in him?

Read Isaiah 53:3–4.

1. In what ways was Christ a "man of sorrows"?

2. **Some versions of the Bible translate part of this verse, "He was . . . acquainted with grief." How does it comfort you to know that Christ knows what grief is all about?**

3. **What does it mean to you that Christ "carried [your] sorrows"?**

Read Hebrews 2:17–18.

1. **Do you feel that Jesus cares and can identify with your pain? Explain.**

2. **Are you isolating from Jesus? In what ways?**

3. **What do you want from him?**

RECOVERY GOALS

The goal of this chapter is to help you gain stability in your grief, to help you do things that bring you nurture and comfort, to allow you to loosen your emotional grip on your loss and begin to do what will help you regain some of your emotional balance.

1. **Are you ready to start taking care of yourself even if you don't feel like it?**

2. When will you begin this process of doing things that bring comfort and love?

3. What are you willing to do on a regular basis to help release the emotional tension that builds up in you? What are you willing to do to help yourself feel better?

4. Whom will you enlist to help you in this process?

5. What unhealthy attitudes and behavior do you need to avoid?

6. How will you do this? When will you begin? Whom will you ask to hold you accountable?

3. The Process of Recovery

RECOVERY FOCUS

- Review the stages of recovery.
- Identify the stage in which you find yourself.
- Find comfort in the Lord.

RECOVERY INFORMATION

Most research that has studied grief recovery divides the process into stages. This book will examine four stages:

Stage 1: letting go or saying good-bye.
Stage 2: an in-between stage; you've said good-bye but haven't begun to move forward.
Stage 3: new definitions, moving from being disoriented to finding a new orientation.
Stage 4: reentry or re-creation, rebuilding the parts that are in change or loss.

Everyone who experiences loss or change moves through these stages. The stages aren't this well defined in real life; they tend to bleed into each other and can be experienced out of order, similar to having a winter-like day in the spring. To further explore the analogy, we could say that fall is the stage of saying good-bye; winter is the in-between time; spring is a time of new definitions; and summer is the time of re-creation fulfilled.

As you move through the grief process, be aware of the dynamics of each stage. You would not want to hinder your recovery by getting stuck in any of these stages.

SAYING GOOD-BYE

If your loss or change was expected, the adjustment is easier than if the loss or change caught you by surprise. Most people experience some shock, numbness, and disorientation as they experience loss or change. Some are even euphoric in the initial stages because the human body releases chemicals to cushion the shock. God created these mechanisms to help us and protect us from the harsh realities of change. Other people may feel a sense of relief, similar to the relief you may have felt when you graduated from school and realized you didn't have to study or be tested anymore.

As you come to terms with saying good-bye to whatever it is you lost—a job, a friend or family member who moved away, a friend or family member who died, a dream, a belief, your health—you face some other difficult issues. Where do you go from here?

Once you make a change or deal with a loss, you may face loneliness, confusion, loss of direction, or purpose. Bill said after retirement, "I used to know what I was going to do every day, and now I feel lost and underfoot. I've looked forward to retirement, but I didn't realize the change would be this difficult."

Jeremy came into counseling complaining that his life was miserable and that he didn't know what he wanted to do with it. He was thirty years old, not married, and working on a graduate degree. He was depressed and had little enthusiasm toward anything. Jeremy's depression was connected to unresolved grief. He had never said good-bye to someone.

Through counseling, Jeremy revealed that he had lost his mother when he was eight years old. She was wonderful to him, the bright spot in his life. After she died, his father sent him to live with an aunt for several years before bringing him back to live with him. In counseling, Jeremy began to express feelings and thoughts with which no one knew he was wrestling. He was writing letters, at the suggestion of his counselor, to his mother. One letter read, "Dear Mom, I wish you would come back. I think about you almost every day and often look for letters in the mailbox from you. At times I'm afraid to move, thinking that maybe I'd miss a letter from you."

Jeremy knew these were irrational thoughts, but he hadn't let go of the hope that his mother would be there for him. He sobbed like a young child when he talked about saying good-bye to his mother. Jeremy realized that he was trying to be a "good boy" and please others so that his mom would come back. During one session he said, "Mom, I need to let go of you. I'll always love you. I've been holding on to the hope of bringing you back, but I need to let go, grow up, and move on with my life. I know this is what you want for me as well." He then faced his grief and said good-bye to his mother, acknowledging that she was gone.

After Jeremy did this, he began to evaluate what he wanted out of life and realized that he really didn't know. So he left graduate school and began to make some very courageous steps to find out what God had for him and what he wanted to do. Although this was a time of seeming inactivity, he was reforming his direction, values, and identity. Jeremy had finished the first step of grief work after twenty-two years of searching for his lost mother. He had said good-bye.

STARTING OVER

You may feel flat after saying good-bye. It may be hard to feel motivated to do anything. Life isn't what you thought it would be. Now you are wrestling with disillusionment. Your frame of reference is changing. You are shedding false images and coming to terms with your own limitations. You vacillate between searching for that which is now gone and looking for something new. You aren't sure what is worth investing in, so you just do what it takes to survive.

You probably will ask lots of questions during this stage: What is real? Who am I now? What's important to me? What's meaningful and worth putting some energy into? Am I going to be hurt again? Will life get better? You don't have the courage to take risks again, and you may not feel strong enough for a while.

Life tends to turn inward during the in-between and new-definitions stages. Then an opportunity enters your life. You've had enough introspection and finishing old business, and you are ready to move on. You want to live again, even if it costs you. You begin to see how God's hand has been there all along. You gain insight that clarifies the ambiguity. Life begins to make some sense again, and you are re-creating.

Rachel was in her last year of medical school and ready to start her internship. She was the model child in her family, and her parents were very proud of her achievements. She had wanted to be a doctor from the time she was six years old. Rachel had been a Christian since childhood and believed that God wanted her to pursue a career in medicine. Three weeks before graduation, Rachel was informed that she was being dropped from medical school. She was devastated.

For the next two years, Rachel attempted to be reinstated to medical school. She alienated her family during that time and fell into a deep depression. For one year she hardly got out of bed. She blamed the medical school and cited many injustices. Her dreams of being a medical doctor were gone, and her identity went with it.

During her year of isolation and alienation, she began to see that her life wasn't over. She began to explore other avenues and reevaluated her own strengths and weaknesses. She decided to apply to a doctoral program that would give her credit for some of her schooling. She received a fellowship and entered school again. This time she graduated with honors and was pursued by many corporations. She took a position that would allow her to help people and use her strengths. Six years after saying good-bye to a career as a medical doctor, she said to her counselor in a letter: "I didn't think my life could have turned out this well. I'm happy in my career and have reestablished my social and spiritual life. The changes were difficult, but now I can see where God was taking me."

RECOVERY PROBERS

1. What are you holding on to and afraid to let go?

2. What will happen if you let go and say good-bye?

3. What needs to be said or done before you can let go?

4. In which of the four stages of recovery are you?

5. Is it okay with you to be where you are in your recovery?

6. **Do you need time just to do nothing?**

7. **In what ways is it difficult to think about who you are and what you are going to do from here?**

RECOVERY GUIDE

A large part of letting go is being able to trust that God is good and has something for you. Sometimes we demand that God express his goodness the way we want it, and we become disappointed when our expectations aren't fulfilled. Trusting is allowing God to guide you through your journey of grief. He knows your sorrow and fears and can be a comfort and surety as you surrender to him. Sometimes God will tell you to let go; sometimes he will tell you to be still and wait. And at other times, God will tell you to step out and take risks.

Read Matthew 26:39.

1. **Did Jesus want to let go?**

2. **How is letting go a process of surrender?**

Read Psalm 27:13–14.

1. **What does it mean for you to wait for the Lord in your present situation?**

2. In what does David base his confidence in waiting for the Lord?

Read Psalm 46:1–3, 10.

1. What does it mean to be still and know that God is God?

2. How does being able to trust in God help you when things around you are unstable?

Read Galatians 6:9.

1. How does this verse relate to rebuilding your life when that stage comes?

2. How does making contributions take faith after a loss or change in your life?

RECOVERY GOALS

The goal of this chapter is to help you understand that recovery is a process. It gives you an overview of some of the stages involved in that process.

1. Where are you in the stages of recovery?

2. How can you trust God in your stage of change?

3. What would keep you stuck and hinder your recovery?

4. Before You Say Good-bye

RECOVERY FOCUS

- Recognize the characteristics of denial.
- Learn why denial is necessary.
- Understand why you can't avoid your loss or change.

RECOVERY INFORMATION

"This can't be happening!" "You must be wrong, doctor!" "What do you mean I've lost my job?" "God wouldn't let that happen to my baby!" "Not another move!" All of these are initial reactions to loss and change.

When you are faced with major loss or change, you will deny the reality of what is happening. You will disbelieve what is happening to you. During this initial phase, before the actual work of grieving begins, you go through denial. And this is appropriate!

Denial comes even when you could anticipate the loss or change. For nearly a year Jenny knew her husband was dying from cancer. Yet when he died, she reported a disbelief and shock that represented her initial denial of his death. A year would appear to be an ample length of time to prepare for the death of a spouse, at least in the minds of many people, but for Jenny that wasn't how she responded.

Gordon knew he would most likely lose his job at the end of the summer. He had been passing his résumé around and had received some good leads for new jobs. In fact, the week before he was given the pink slip, he had a solid job offer in a new and challenging field of work that interested him. But when he actually got the pink slip, he sat down confused and a little dazed. He hadn't realized this would bother him. He felt different from how he had imagined he would feel.

Denial protects us initially from the shock created by the loss or change. Without the initial disbelief that accompanies most losses, we would find ourselves overwhelmed by the reality of the change. Some characteristics common to denial include *shock, disbelief, numbness, unusual energy,* and *relief.* Let's take a brief look at each of these characteristics.

SHOCK

Ron's daughter died in a tragic accident. The first few days after her death, he felt a euphoria that he reported was "God sparing me from the grief of losing my baby." He believed that he would not grieve! However, this euphoria gave way to depression and anger that took Ron nearly three years to work through.

God has created us in such a way that shock becomes the body's defense against the emotional overload that the news of a loss or change can create. People recall feeling an anesthetized high that sustained them through the initial hours, days, and sometimes weeks after their loss. This is God's way of protecting us from the initial onslaught of trauma that we must work through later.

DISBELIEF

Henry had spent the last fifteen years climbing the corporate ladder. He had worked as hard as he knew how. He saw himself as a valuable team player, and his efforts had been rewarded numerous times with promotions and pay raises. Then Henry lost his job. He went from a large salary and a prestigious position to nothing. And now nobody wanted him. He was jobless and had no prospects. He felt helpless and dazed. Henry recounted that he felt as if his situation was unreal, as if it wasn't happening, even though he knew it was. He had come to believe that his hard work would insulate him from the tragedy of the unemployment he now faced.

Initial disbelief allows the opportunity to work gradually through loss or change. In the beginning disbelief helps people continue to function.

NUMBNESS

When Janice moved to another state to get married, she lost all her job contacts and friends. The move was necessary, and she wanted very much to be married, but the change was more difficult than she initially had predicted. For some time after the move, she felt empty and numb. She told her fiancé that she couldn't feel good or bad, that it was difficult to feel anything at all. This created adjustment problems in her new marriage.

What often happens when we become numb is that we distance ourselves emotionally and spiritually from ourselves. This guards us against feeling the pain of our loss or change, but it also keeps us from feeling anything at all.

UNUSUAL ENERGY

Excessive stress triggers the body's "fight-or-flight" mode. Our bodies become aroused, pumping into our systems hormones that give us the ability to defend ourselves. Our palms sweat, we shake, our appetites are suppressed, and our sleep is disrupted. Our world becomes a threatening place in which to live. The constants in our lives have been so disrupted that we naturally fear what might happen next. Nothing seems stable. Our body is ready to do battle (fight), run (flight), or do both.

JoAnne, a recent widow, had to be doing something constantly. Sitting was difficult. She would begin a task, then drop it only to start another. She washed every pan in the house twice. When she arrived at the store, she forgot what she went shopping for. She went to the doctor to complain of muscle tension and back pain as well as headaches. She told her sister that it seemed as if time was flying by. She felt scared much of the time, especially when she was left alone.

Tom knew his wife wanted a divorce. She had spoken to him about it on several occasions. Each time he would avoid the subject. When his wife became angry and threatened divorce, Tom could sense his anxiety level rise. He felt panicky and restless. His mouth became dry, and he could feel himself tense up and begin to shake. He would take a walk but would be unable to relax or focus his thoughts.

RELIEF

Many people report feeling relief during the denial phase. They say there is a feeling of relief that seems to give them a natural high or euphoria.

Everyone said Mary seemed so strong throughout the funeral and the days that followed. Later, Mary said she felt relieved rather than sad at her mother's death. Her mom had suffered from Alzheimer's disease for three years. The burden of caring for her mother had taxed Mary's patience and faith. She felt guilty because of her sense of relief.

Donald felt relieved for nine months after his wife had left him. He saw himself as being liberated from a sick and repressive marriage. The day he received the final papers in the mail, however, he was overwhelmed at the reality of what had happened. He cried every day for two weeks. Don's denial protected him from the reality of the death of his marriage. It wasn't until it was final that he began grieving over the loss.

Each of these characteristics of denial is a normal response to the significant losses and changes we all face in life. Denial can be healthy. Denial is appropriate, a God-given response to the overwhelming pain that significant losses and changes produce. Almost all people who experience loss deny, at least partially, the reality of what has happened. Denial acts as an anesthetic, providing a brief relief from the reality you must ultimately face. It's a defense that helps you collect yourself and gain strength to face the reality of your loss. People are often pushed too quickly out of their denial. However, many times they need permission to protect themselves from overwhelming losses and changes. Denial protects you until you are ready to begin to feel. Don't feel guilty because of your denial.

It's only when denial *persists* that it becomes unhealthy. If you continue to avoid facing the grief created by the changes and losses in your life, you rob yourself of the opportunity to be healed. Jesus said in the Sermon on the Mount, "Blessed are those who mourn, for they will be comforted" (Matt. 5:4). When you avoid the mourning process or the process of working through the stages of your grief, you are less likely to find comfort.

THE STOIC RESPONSE

Avoiding grief is not a new phenomenon. The ancient stoic philosophers viewed grieving or mourning as a weakness. The stoics believed in a concept called the undisturbed, wise, or virtuous man. This person was one who was strong, logical, rational, and self-controlled. A stoic was to respond to grief with self-control, no tears, no mourning.

Grief has been stigmatized by this stoic response. We somehow view the grieving process as a weakness or a mental illness. Our culture places even heavier burdens on men, who are taught not to cry. Some people view grieving as unchristian. Somehow, the logic goes, our Christian faith insulates us from grief. When a death occurs, for example, we are to rejoice that our loved one is now in heaven with God. But Christians are supposed to grieve! We can't help but grieve. To avoid and ignore what we feel only serves to make our grief work more difficult in the future. Christ responded to his grief by weeping when his friend Lazarus died (John 11:35). We too can give ourselves permission to work through our grief, but only by facing it. Avoidance will only increase our sorrow. The stoic response isn't a godly one.

A young youth pastor was faced with a tragic auto accident in which one of the young people in his church's youth group was killed. At the funeral, many of the young people who were close to the girl who had died were sobbing. The youth pastor became visibly angered and later confronted the group about the inappropriateness of their response. He felt their theology was wrong. This girl was now in heaven. Why cry? What this young man didn't recognize was the inadequacy of his own theology. He had taken the view of the stoics: control your emotions, be strong, don't weep. This is a perverted form of denial. The young people needed to cry, and so did this youth pastor. Tears are part of God's created mechanism to express grief.

After the initial period of denial, it's essential to *work through* your grief. Yet our society often minimizes the work that grief takes (as well as its benefits). It's only in working through your grief that you will emerge as a new person. Times of grief give God the opportunity to mold and shape your character in unexpected ways.

When as a culture we underestimate the need to do grief work, we encourage people to deny the reality of what has happened to them. And we hinder the ultimate growth and healing that God gives as we work through our grief.

There are no shortcuts in the grieving process. When your friends or family are in grief, you may want to relieve the pain of their loss or change. Or you may wish somehow to cut corners in your own painful grief work. But what you need to understand is that you can't circumvent the grieving process. Directly facing your loss—with all the hurt, anger, guilt, and shame that accompanies it—is the healthiest and most Christian response you can have.

RECOVERY PROBERS

1. **Did you anticipate your change or loss, or were you surprised by it? How does this affect your denial?**

2. **How does denial protect you initially after your loss?**

3. Which characteristics of denial (shock, disbelief, numbness, unusual energy, or relief) best describe your situation? Why?

4. Why do you think avoiding grief is a common response?

5. What scares you the most about facing your loss?

6. What has been the most difficult roadblock as you have worked to overcome your denial?

7. Why do Christians grieve just like those who don't have their faith in Christ?

RECOVERY GUIDE

Read 2 Samuel 12:15–17.

1. King David's initial response to the news that his child would die was one of denial. What were the characteristics of David's denial?

2. **David bargained and pleaded with God. Have you attempted to strike a bargain with God in the hopes of reversing your loss?**

Read 1 Thessalonians 4:13–14.

The pagans ("the rest of men, who have no hope") at the time of Christ believed that death was the end of it all. There was nothing beyond death. There was a permanency, a finality to the death of those without Christ.

1. **How might this passage be easily misinterpreted?**

2. **How could a misinterpretation of this passage keep you in denial of your loss?**

RECOVERY GOALS

This chapter's goal is to help you understand the normalcy of denial. Denial is only the beginning of a long grieving process that we all must work through to achieve healing.

1. **How has your denial been a normal response to your loss?**

5. Saying Good-bye

RECOVERY FOCUS

- Examine the characteristics of the saying-good-bye stage.
- Recognize which characteristics you have experienced.
- Understand how you learn to say good-bye through experiencing these characteristics.

RECOVERY INFORMATION

Denial isn't something you experience briefly and then never experience again. As you begin the tough process of saying good-bye to whomever or whatever you've lost, you'll find yourself in moments of disbelief and confusion over what has happened. You need not see these interludes of denial as setbacks in your grief work. Brief periods of denial are normal during this stage of saying good-bye.

Several characteristics define this stage of grief work: *preoccupation with the loss or change, grief attacks, searching, emotional overload, sensing and dreaming, faith questioning,* and *marathon stress.* You may not experience all these characteristics. And you will experience them at varying degrees of intensity.

PREOCCUPATION WITH LOSS OR CHANGE

Sue Ellen's daughter died of cancer at the age of nine. Every night Sue Ellen rehearsed all the good times she had with her daughter in those nine years. As Sue Ellen reviewed the events over and over in her mind, her emotions would become stirred up, and she would cry herself to sleep. Sue Ellen couldn't get her daughter's death out of her mind. She saw her lying in the hospital bed in pain. She would remember caring for her. She would think of the funeral. Sue Ellen was uncontrollably preoccupied with her loss.

Bill's divorce had been final for three months. His close friend Rob couldn't understand why Bill continued to talk incessantly about his former wife. Sometimes Rob would catch Bill saying "my wife" instead of "my ex-wife."

When Jenny's company transferred her from one part of the country to another, she was glad she still had a job. But the cross-country change had been more difficult than she had anticipated. She found herself obsessively thinking about her old job and home.

Each of these people illustrates the initial difficulties we face in saying good-bye. They intellectually recognized the loss but emotionally didn't acknowledge it.

Many people report a heightened fear and anxiety as they thought about their loss or change. C. S. Lewis wrote in *A Grief Observed* of his fear when his wife died. He said that his experience of grief felt very much like fear, even though he didn't think he was afraid.

This fixation on our loss can keep us from saying good-bye and moving on with our lives. In the case of Sue Ellen, she had continued her nightly ritual of review for seven years. She was afraid to say good-bye. Linda had a similar experience. She lost her husband in a boating accident. It took her a number of years to end her preoccupation with her husband. She believed that he would somehow come back.

GRIEF ATTACKS

Ron felt he was doing better with his grief. But he did find himself having grief attacks, which confused him greatly. When he walked into a grocery store, he realized that he used to do this with his former wife and that he would never shop with her again. Without warning he was overcome with grief. The pain was similar to the initial pain of his divorce, almost too much to bear.

Jan would go to church and see somebody with a baby and become so overwhelmed with the pain of the loss of her own baby that she would have to find a quiet place and pray until the grief attack subsided before she could attend the worship service.

Grief attacks are normal experiences in saying good-bye to our losses and changes. They can be set off by the smell of your deceased wife's perfume or the smell of cut grass, a chore that your former husband used to do. The smallest things can trigger a grief attack. When they occur, take time to name your feelings, give them to God in prayer, and consider your actions before you move on with your daily routine.

SEARCHING

Many people experience a strong desire to search for the lost person or thing. This is particularly true when the loss is a result of death. They may intellectually realize it's irrational to search for a dead spouse, child, or parent, yet they will think they see the deceased person while shopping at the mall. They aren't often actively aware of their searching behavior until they catch themselves in the act.

People can also search for lost dreams, lost ideals, or a lost sense of self. Bill spent years putting together a successful business only to see it fall apart. He spent six months figuring out a way to make his bankrupt company work again, even though all his associates told him it was lost.

Brenda was a super athlete in high school and college. In her forties, however, she grieved the deterioration of her body. The years and three children had taken their toll. She searched for her old self by working hard to enter a competition she had no hope of winning.

Don's son died of leukemia. Every once in a while Don found himself thinking he heard his son playing in the backyard. And once Don thought he saw him at the park playing baseball with his friends.

Belinda would go to her mailbox everyday, hoping that her mother had sent her a letter. She knew her mother had died, but she found herself unable to stop from checking the mailbox with anticipation anyway.

Often this searching is difficult to admit to others because it appears so irrational. Searching is a normal part of saying good-bye; it's only when this behavior persists that it presents a problem. Belinda's searching was destructive. Her mailbox behavior had kept her from saying good-bye to her mother, who had died when Belinda was twelve years old. For twenty years Belinda had been unable to say good-bye. Her chronic grief had blocked the healing of her loss.

EMOTIONAL OVERLOAD

Saying good-bye to a loss or change requires a large amount of emotional and spiritual energy. "Losing my job was such a surprise. It turned my world upside down," stated Lois. She was sure her world would never be the same. All of her emotional responses had been intensified. She became depressed more easily, and her tolerance level was much lower. If the smallest thing went wrong, she became frustrated and anxious. She would cry without provocation, feel overwhelming guilt for not providing adequately for her children, and could never get over the cold she had gotten shortly after she had been fired. She had always had a problem with anger, but after her job loss, she felt mad at everyone. Lois was experiencing emotional overload. Her doctor prescribed a temporary medication to get her through this period, and the counseling center at her church provided some relief from her overload.

SENSING AND DREAMING

As you work through your grief, you may sense the presence of the person or thing you lost. Marsha walked into her house and thought she saw her former husband in the living room. Jake woke up one night sensing that his deceased wife was in bed next to him. Maria told her pastor she saw Debra, her child who had died in an accident, playing in the backyard with her older sister. Some people find these experiences eerie and almost scary, while others report them to be of some comfort.

Another normal and common experience is dreaming about the loss. George kept dreaming that when he picked up the phone, his former boss would be on the other end, offering him his old job back. Cathy's dream felt so real that when she woke up she was sure John was in the room with her. Through most of the next day, Cathy couldn't shake the feeling that John was somehow alive and close by. And this happened on more than one occasion.

FAITH QUESTIONING

As you work to say good-bye to your loss or change, you may feel an intense need to question why, to make sense out of what has happened. During the initial phase of this searching process, you feel a sense of unfairness. Life has been unjust. You've done the best you could in living your life, but it hasn't paid off. You may be mad at God. Jennie's fiancé died in a car accident as he was on the way to their wedding ceremony. She felt her Christian faith had somehow failed her. She felt God had betrayed her.

Mike's wife left him after her affair. His Christian belief system was knocked out from underneath him. His perceptions about how the Christian life was to be lived had been turned upside down. His confusion led to bitterness toward God. He felt an injustice had been done to him by God. Mike had certain expectations of his Christian life. He was under the illusion that if he lived a certain way, God would protect him from this sort of loss. When she left, he became disillusioned.

The feelings of unfairness and the confusion over your Christian faith are common responses to loss. God is big enough for your questions, your doubts, and even your anger. You can go to him and yell and scream. He will be there to listen, and he *will* answer, even though his answer may not be on your timetable.

Unfortunately, many of the things well-intentioned Christians say contribute to your doubts. Mark was told after the death of his son that it was God's will. People want so much to have life organized and figured out that a tragedy doesn't fit into their world view. Believing that a death or other significant loss is part of God's perfect plan helps them organize the chaos and evil present in our world. What you, the grieving person, need to hear instead is how awful and tragic your loss really is. When others say things like it was God's will, they are unintentionally blaming God. And when this happens, you may be tempted to blame him too.

MARATHON STRESS

Life's losses complicate your life. And these complications burden you with additional stress. Losses leave you with additional decisions and extra work that needs to be done. This creates more conflict in your life. Norma's husband was a cocaine addict. She hadn't known until she caught him. She subsequently learned that he had used all their savings and had refinanced their home to pay for his cocaine. He abandoned the family, leaving her with two kids and all the debt. Her life was stressed.

After Kate died, Jim had to care for their three children, work his fifty-hour-a-week job, and manage the household, doing tasks he had never done before, like cooking meals, shopping, and doing the laundry. And he had to do all this while mourning the loss of his beloved wife.

Loss and change almost always produce physical symptoms. Stress lowers the resistance of your immune system, making you more susceptible to illness. Your stress may lead to incessant headaches, or you may develop an ulcer or have insomnia.

LETTING YOURSELF FEEL

Saying good-bye to your loss or change involves letting yourself feel. As you become more and more aware of your loss, you move out of denial and confront your grief. You haven't wanted to feel because feeling embraces the reality of the loss. But every time you do feel, you are learning to say good-bye.

None of the characteristics described here are abnormal or unchristian. They are an expected part of the process of saying good-bye. This is a learning stage in which you learn to deal with loss.

When you find yourself preoccupied with memories of your dead parents, you are learning and realizing that they are gone. When you are overcome with grief attacks over your divorce, you are learning to remember that you are no longer married. When you search for your lost child, you are being taught that the child is dead and will not be found. When you feel overwhelmed and controlled by anger or guilt or depression, you are offered another opportunity to learn you have experienced a change or a loss. When you sense the presence or dream of your deceased spouse, you find yourself a student in the school of grief. Your anger at God and your doubts about your Christian faith can also teach you that your loss or change is a reality. And yes, as you cope with and lessen the stress in your life, you learn of the need to say good-bye.

This learning process takes time. You will not want to feel all the pain of your loss or change quickly. Remember, there are no shortcuts to your grief work. Often you may find yourself feeling much better, only to be overwhelmed again by grief. You may feel as if you are going crazy, that something is wrong with you. This is when you need a support group and trusted friends. Talking with others who have experienced grief similar to yours can help you learn to say good-bye to your change or loss.

No timetable can help you determine exactly how long it will take to learn that your loss is real. For some people saying good-bye takes six months, while for others it may take two years. You probably will go through a cycle of initial denial followed by intense grief as you begin to learn to say good-bye. This intensity will diminish and then return. Your grief will probably follow this cycle of intensity and stabilization for some time.

If you feel at any time that you are stuck in your grief, find professional help from your minister, physician, or a qualified counselor. Don't be afraid to ask for the help and assistance you believe you need. It's all too easy to isolate yourself from others, yet you need social support now more than ever. Actively seek out social and spiritual support. Maintain your contact with God and Christians. Find a self-help group for those experiencing loss or change.

RECOVERY PROBERS

1. How have you regressed into denial or partial denial as you have begun the process of saying good-bye?

2. In what ways have you been preoccupied with your loss or change?

3. How often have you experienced a grief attack? Describe what usually happens.

4. What emotions seem to overwhelm you in your grief?

5. Have you sensed the presence of a lost spouse or dreamed about the lost person? Describe your experiences.

6. In what ways have you questioned your faith since your loss or change?

7. **How has your loss or change contributed to more stress in your life?**

8. **How are the aspects of the saying-good-bye stage (preoccupation, grief attacks, searching, emotional overload, sensing and dreaming, faith questioning, and marathon stress) helping you learn to say good-bye?**

RECOVERY GUIDE

Read Genesis 50:1–11.

1. **What mourning ritual did Joseph and his family and community perform?**

2. **How did that ritual help the people say good-bye to their loved one?**

3. **What can you learn from this ritual? What part (if any) of this ritual would be helpful for you?**

Read 2 Samuel 1:11–12.

1. What mourning rituals did David and his men perform?

2. What value did the tearing of their clothes have for the mourners?

Read 2 Samuel 13:19.

1. What mourning rituals did Tamar perform?

2. What value did ashes on her head have for Tamar and for the people who would see her?

Read Ezra 10:1, 6.

1. What mourning rituals did Ezra perform?

2. In what way did the community join him in his mourning?

Read Esther 4:1, 3.

1. **What mourning rituals did Mordecai and the Jews perform?**

2. **What function did the sackcloth (a coarse and uncomfortable cloth) play in the mourning process?**

3. **What was helpful about the loud wailing and crying?**

4. **What can you learn from this ritual? What part (if any) of this ritual would be helpful for you?**

Read Job 3.

This passage describes the anguish Job felt as a result of his losses. He wished he had never been born. He can't understand what has happened to him. Job is not in denial over his losses. He has embraced his feelings and cries out in pain. He comes close to cursing God. He longs for peace in his life, a serenity he feels he will not find. Verse 16 finds Job wishing that he would have been dead at birth. Since Job was born, his second choice or wish was that he would have been born dead. That way his soul would now be in the grave and at rest.

1. How have you felt like Job?

2. Why do you think it is normal to want to escape the pain of grief?

RECOVERY GOALS

The goal of this chapter is to get you to own your grief. This means you begin to feel your pain. Each time you feel the pain of your loss, you are saying good-bye.

1. How have you begun to say good-bye to what you lost?

2. How has allowing yourself to express your feelings helped you in the good-bye process?

3. What rituals can you create to help you work through your grief? (Examples: watch a sad movie with a friend and cry together; take thirty minutes every morning to cry over your loss; drive your car to a secluded area and wail for as long as you need to.)

4. How can you use the characteristics of this stage to help you learn to say good-bye (preoccupation, grief attacks, searching, emotional overload, sensing and dreaming, faith questioning, stress)?

6. Recognition or Resignation?

RECOVERY FOCUS

- Learn why grieving is difficult today.
- Understand the choices you have in your grieving.
- Discover positive methods of actively working through your grief.

RECOVERY INFORMATION

Grieving loss and change is difficult work. In some ways it has always been difficult. Yet in other ways, significant changes since World War II have contributed to the increased difficulty we face in grieving.

In the past, people had deep social and spiritual supports provided by lifelong community and church ties. Those deep ties are not a part of our lives today. We move from city to city, from state to state. Maybe we have made some good friends in the area in which we live, but that's not always the case. Meaningful relationships take time to build; we have to be much more intentional in creating communities of support in our neighborhood, school, church, and even family lives. When we grieve a loss today, we often do it in the midst of strangers, not people who knew our families before we were born.

In the past, death and loss were more an expected part of life. Women and infants often died in childbirth; children died from pneumonia; people died of heart attacks. These were accepted losses. But with ultrasound technology, fetal monitors, and Caesarean sections, women and children rarely die in childbirth in our culture. With X-ray technology and antibiotic therapy, children rarely die from pneumonia in our culture. In our cholesterol-conscious society with its technical ability to do by-pass surgeries and transplants, people die less frequently from heart attacks. The point is this: We have come to expect medical technology to stave off death. We have refused to accept the realities and normalcy of death and loss. This makes our grieving more difficult.

Our grieving is also made difficult by the complex lives we live. When we lose something significant—a loved one, a job, or a limb—we must not only say good-bye to it, but also say good-bye to the secondary things associated with what we've lost. When Hector lost his job, he not only had to say good-bye to fifteen years of employment at a career he loved but also had to say good-bye to certain friends, status, and dreams. When Ann's husband died at the age of forty-two, she lost more than a spouse. She lost a comfortable income, someone who helped raise two children, the status that went along with being a physician's wife, a spiritual soul mate—and the list goes on. What we often fail to recognize is the fact that we are grieving over more than just our primary losses or changes. We are also saying good-bye to all those secondary things that accompanied the primary one.

CHOICES

In spite of the difficulties you face in your grief, you must do the work of grieving. In the beginning of your grief work, you *reacted* to your losses or changes. You initially denied what happened, disbelieving that "this" could happen to you. You felt strong emotional and spiritual reactions such as anger, guilt, and depression. You may have been mad at God and blamed him or questioned his love and involvement in your life. You have longed for and even searched out your lost loved one or thing. You have wished and wished that things could be as they had been in the past. Your anxiety has intensified to where, at times, you thought you might be going crazy.

These are normal emotional and spiritual reactions. The emphasis here is on *reactions*. You have been responding to how you felt. You have allowed yourself to feel, as painful as that has been. The grief work you have done so far hasn't been self-initiated. What you have been through is a normal response that all people go through as they begin to say good-bye. Now you must make some very concrete *choices* about your loss or change. You must do the initiating in your grief work.

In most cases, you didn't choose to experience this loss or change. You have simply experienced the pain, anguish, and sorrow that your loss or change has created in your life. Up to this point, you couldn't do much except react.

Yet, now that you are in the midst of the process of grieving, you have several choices. You can make healthy choices or unhealthy ones.

Maybe you will choose to fight the loss or change; in doing so you decide not to release the past or consider a new way of living. Maybe you will choose to resign yourself intellectually to the loss or change, but emotionally you will not give it up. Maybe you will choose to stay invested in what you have lost; you may feel that to acknowledge and accept the loss means you will never get back what you have lost. Or perhaps the thought of recognizing the loss or change produces more guilt and shame than you can bear. You may feel disloyal if you move on with your life. Or by not saying good-bye, you leave the door open to get back what you have lost.

Five years after her divorce, Betty was still stuck in her grief. She refused to give up hope that her former husband would return to her. When he married again, it was more than she could bear. Her pastor referred her to a counselor, who at one point almost hospitalized Betty because of her suicidal thoughts. Looking back, Betty sees how she was unwilling to say good-bye to twenty-two years of marriage. Her refusal to relinquish her past marriage prolonged her grief and kept her from healing. "I wish I could have said good-bye earlier. I know I needed to grieve, but I didn't want to go through it. I avoided it." Betty believed that somehow God would convict her husband of his sin and bring him back to her. She put her life on hold for five years, waiting and praying for this to happen.

We aren't saying here that you give your faith up. God sometimes does intervene, and miraculous healings in marriages occur. What we would like to point out is that many times you confuse faith with denial. Betty continued to deny the reality of her lost marriage. She didn't want to look objectively at her situation or listen to the counsel of Christians in her life.

Laura said she didn't want to go on with her life after her son died of leukemia. "There's nothing I can do about it. I guess I have to go on living since I don't have any other choice." Laura saw no hope in her situation and didn't want to look for any. She had resigned herself to the loss of her son but was unwilling to accept it. In this way she has never fully recognized her loss. She has silently suffered through her pain and will continue to be stuck as long as she chooses resignation over acceptance.

Laura, Betty, and many others have made unhealthy choices, and these choices have left them stuck. You have other options. You can make healthy choices.

You can choose to recognize the reality of your loss and accept it. When you simply react to your grief, you never fully finish the work of grief. In one sense you will never finish; you will always remember your loss. But in another sense you can complete your grief work. You can choose to work through your grief more actively. You can recognize that your loss is real and that you are ready to go on with your life in a new way. You can own your loss or change.

Dorothy's kids had all moved out. She now knew what people meant by the "empty nest." When two of her kids came home from college for the Christmas break, she saw evidence of how God was working in their lives. She realized they were both in good places in their own lives. She said it wasn't easy letting go at first, but she was able to be glad when they returned to school. She had ***recognized*** and accepted the loss of her parent role. If she had only ***resigned*** herself to this loss, she would have said something like "If it has to be this way, it has to be." Instead, she saw the good in their leaving and was now ready to move to a new stage in her life.

Don't expect this acceptance to come easily. Who likes to think that they will ever readily accept their mastectomy, divorce, job loss, move, or loss of a child? Grief is painful stuff. Recognition may seem impossible at first. But as you choose to actively work through your grief, you will find yourself reaching a turning point in your life. The pain will begin to subside. You will find God providing you the strength to make more constructive decisions that help you actively work through your feelings. You begin to recognize that you can't go back to life the way it was. You will find yourself no longer searching for your former spouse or yearning so desperately for a dead loved one. You will be able to thank them for the good times and recognize that the bad times were hard and say good-bye.

WORKING THROUGH GRIEF POSITIVELY

Take care of unfinished business. In many losses and changes there is unfinished business. Taking care of these loose ends is one active way you can choose to recognize and accept a loss. Any issue that you feel wasn't addressed before the loss is an example of unfinished business. Whatever you feel is unresolved can block your ability to recognize the loss. Perhaps you never were able to share some hurt or resentment with your father before he died. Or you know you needed to deal with some anger or unresolved disagreement. Maybe you had some regrets you needed to share. Possibly you needed to confess a past sin. Or perhaps great harm was done to you. Maybe you just needed to say good-bye or I love you. Whatever your unfinished business is, you will probably find that actively taking care of it now can help you say good-bye and get on with your life.

Many grieving people have found great help in writing a letter to outline their unfinished business. This is a letter you don't intend to mail to anyone. By writing down how you feel, what you have done, your responsibility in the unfinished business, and what you wish might have been, you are actively choosing to work through your grief. Perhaps you will choose to keep the letter to yourself. Or you may decide to share your letter with a friend or with a support group.

Write a good-bye to your grief. Many people find it helpful to write out a good-bye letter to whomever or whatever they have lost. As you write the letter, you will experience very painful emotions. It may take several sessions to complete. It also may take more than one letter. But the method is an active way to move through your grief and say good-bye. Actually writing good-bye in the letter can go a long way toward moving on with the next phase of your life. You may decide to read the letter every day for a week. This can help reinforce the saying-good-bye process.

Reframe your pain. Look at what happened to you in a new way. Jim had been fired from his job. He struggled with the guilt of not working when his wife was six months pregnant. But looking back on the experience a year later, Jim could see how his old job had controlled him. He had physical symptoms of stress, he had gained weight, and his marriage was beginning to experience trouble. His marriage problems were one of the main reasons he had agreed to start a family. In looking at his loss in a new way, Jim saw that God used his job loss to change his priorities. Jim got a less-demanding job, and even though it paid less than his previous job, it gave him more time for his son and new energy in his marriage. In reframing his pain, Jim could begin to see how God has been at work within his loss.

Roger had spent fourteen years building up a business that eventually went bankrupt. His success had created a monster. He had escalated his lifestyle at the expense of his spiritual life. It had cost him his marriage and time with his kids. Now three years later Roger has a new perspective on what happened. He sees how God worked through his financial troubles to teach him surrender and obedience. Roger has realized what is really important in life.

Jonathan broke his back and found himself in a wheelchair. After a protracted grieving period, he viewed his condition in a more positive light. Instead of complaining about being crippled, he realized that he could spend more time with his kids. Family conflicts were substantially reduced, and he was happier. His wife also was happier in her career knowing that Jonathan was home with the children.

When you reframe your pain, you begin to see yourself, God, and others in a new way. You begin to turn the corner in your grief work from response to action.

We often fight letting go, wanting to control our losses. But holding onto our grief keeps us from accepting a new way of looking at the situation. In time, you will begin to reframe your loss as you work through your grief.

Think of it this way. When young children move from their cribs to beds, they can feel like Chicken Little (the sky is falling), that all is lost. Yet, we as adults see the change from a different vantage point. We realize the children are physically outgrowing their cribs, that it could prove to be dangerous if they remained in them. Young children can't see this, however. They can only respond to their feelings. When we can begin to get a new perspective, we can see how God is working through our losses and changes. And we can then be open to seeing what he has for us to learn.

Recognize and verbalize your needs. Asking for what you need is another important and active approach to grief work. You often isolate yourself rather than ask for help. But support from others can help you keep your perspective on life. You need the nurturing and help of others to keep you working through your grief. Spend time with people who will listen and talk with you as you work through your grief. Identify what you feel you need, and then begin to ask others for assistance.

Jane's husband had been dead for three years. She felt excluded from many of the social activities she and her husband had participated in together. Yet she never asked to be included in any of these, assuming she wouldn't be welcomed. However, once she realized she needed these social interactions and asked her friends to invite her, she felt very welcomed.

Two years after his son had been killed in a car accident, Jerry was angry at the members of his Sunday school class. His class had shown their concern initially, then quit asking Jerry about his son. Jerry still felt he needed to talk about his loss but didn't sense it was safe to do so. Perhaps if Jerry voiced his concern and anger, the class would again show interest in his loss and help him mourn.

RECOVERY PROBERS

1. How has today's world made your grief more difficult to bear?

2. In addition to your primary loss or change, what secondary losses have you experienced?

3. Why must you go through the painful process of grieving?

4. What might happen to you if you continue only to react to your grief?

5. How ready are you to move from reacting to your grief to working through your grief actively?

6. What does it mean to you to recognize the reality of your loss or change?

7. Why is accepting the reality of your loss or change so painful?

8. What unfinished business needs to get finished?

9. How can you reframe your loss or change to give it a new perspective?

RECOVERY GUIDE

Read Romans 8:28.

1. How might God be working through your loss or change for the good?

2. Why is it okay to *feel* that your loss or change isn't working for the good even though you see that it is?

3. How can you be more open to seeing your situation from God's perspective?

Read Proverbs 16:4.

1. **In what ways is it difficult for you to see God working through your loss or change? Why is it hard?**

2. **When you look at your situation from God's perspective, what new meaning does your situation take on?**

Read Genesis 50:20.

1. **Joseph had experienced many losses in his life: his brothers hated him and sold him into slavery; he had to leave the land of his father; he landed in jail for an unjust accusation. How does Joseph reframe his losses in this verse?**

2. **How does Joseph's statement reflect his confidence in God's sovereignty?**

RECOVERY GOALS

The goal of this chapter is to help you accept your loss or change. Out of this acceptance comes a new sense of hope for the future.

1. **What makes you think you have begun to accept your loss or change?**

2. **How are you beginning to feel hopeful about your future?**

3. **What unhealthy choices have you made in working through your grief?**

4. **What healthy choices will you begin to make?**

5. **What needs do you have in your loss? Whom can you ask to help you meet those needs?**

6. **Write a letter saying good-bye to your loss.**

7. Unhealthy Grief

RECOVERY FOCUS

- Avoid isolation.
- Suspend judgment about God.
- Move away from unhealthy grief.

RECOVERY INFORMATION

Grief can overwhelm you with strong feelings. The danger is that these feelings can lead you to make unhealthy decisions. You may feel tempted to isolate from others because of your hurt; you're afraid that you might somehow get hurt, and you know you can't deal with any more pain. This temptation to isolate yourself is a normal feeling that comes from grief. But if you allow those feelings to cut you off from other people or God, you are making an unhealthy decision.

ALIENATION AND ISOLATION

Alienation is a by-product of the change process. To become alienated means to lose a connection and feel as if you no longer belong. Often hostile or unfriendly feelings accompany it.

A childhood song defines alienation like this: "Nobody loves me, everybody hates me. I'm sittin' in the garden eating worms." When you go through grief, you can become alienated from other people, yourself, and God. You have a difficult time making connections because of the intensity of your feelings. When you don't feel loved, comforted, or acknowledged in your grief, it upsets you even more.

It's important to keep your connections during times of change. This may be hard because people may say the wrong things to you, making it harder for you to feel close to them. They may say things that aren't helpful, like, "God has a purpose in this." This may be true, but your pain may make you only angry when they say this. Their statements may communicate insensitivity, even though their intentions are good. They may say, "I know how you feel." Again, you may feel only anger because they can't possibly know how you feel!

It's helpful for you as well as your friends and family if you define how they can help you. You may need a friend just to be with you in your pain and not say anything to try to make you feel better. Say, "Marilyn, I know it's not pleasant for you to hear me say these angry [or sad or confused or resentful] things every day, but it helps me so much when you listen to me. Somehow hearing myself say the words to you takes away some of the sting."

If your friends and family are uncomfortable with your anger or sadness, let them know that you won't always be this way. Again, talk to them. Say, "I know you don't understand my anger with God about this loss, but that's where I am today. I hope that someday I'll be beyond this, but for today, the anger is still strong. Don't be afraid that I've lost my faith because I say these things; just listen to me while I go through this phase. It helps me so much to know that you will listen. I don't expect you to fix my situation. I don't expect you to fix my anger. I don't expect you to argue with me. Just let me be in this place today."

Your grief may cause you to alienate from yourself. You may blame yourself for the loss or change. The shame, guilt, and blame cause you to feel alienated. This can keep you from moving on in the grief process. You may become compulsive in doing sacrificial things to appease your guilt. You may receive neglect or abuse from others to appease your shame.

Jeff had been suffering for seventeen years with hidden guilt. The weekend before his wife was killed in a car accident, he had slept with another woman. He felt that God had punished him for this affair and was ashamed. For seventeen years Jeff had felt that her death was his fault.

Soon after his wife's death, Jeff married to provide a mother for his son. Jeff's new wife was verbally abusive and distant, which he tried to ignore until his son was old enough to leave home. It was then that Jeff realized he was unhappy with the marriage, and he went to counseling. Through counseling Jeff was able to face himself and deal with the guilt over the loss of his first wife. He resisted improving the marriage because he felt he didn't deserve to find happiness.

He prayed and asked God to help him receive forgiveness so he could let go of his anger and shame toward himself. He worked until he was able to forgive himself. He felt tremendous relief in releasing his guilt and in forgiving himself.

Alienation from God is sometimes harder to admit in times of grief. Most people who have been trusting in God feel some alienation during painful times. Jesus described John the Baptist as one of the great men of all times, but when he was in prison even John began to doubt Christ.

The pain of grief pushes you toward several conclusions about God. It feels as if God isn't a good God. It feels as if God isn't there as you cry out. It feels as if God isn't fair. These feelings can lead you to decisions that can cut you off from God and leave you even more isolated.

Os Guinness addresses these struggles in his book *In Two Minds*. His answer to this dilemma of faith is that you can "suspend judgment." This means that you don't have to make a decision based on your feelings that God isn't good, fair, or there for you. You have other evidence and experience that you can use to suspend judgment.

Suspending judgment is saying, "I don't know why God allows this pain and suffering, and it feels as if he doesn't care, but my feelings can change. I'm not going to be angry and sad forever." By suspending the conclusions that your feelings lead you to, you can be real with your feelings, intellectually honest, and not lose your faith.

Our experiences in life don't necessarily reflect directly on God. Jesus felt deep grief and felt as if God had abandoned him when he was on the cross, "My God, My God, why have you forsaken me?" (Mark 15:34).

God isn't surprised by your feelings of anger and deep sadness during times of grief, and he's not offended by your doubt. That's a normal part of working through the pain of grief and letting go. The danger is in making decisions that would turn you away from God's love.

GETTING STUCK AND UNSTUCK

Grief is primarily an emotional issue. It can also make you regress to feeling and acting like a child. You may feel like taking your ball and going home, wanting never to come out and play again. You may fixate on your loss, become angry and resentful, hoping what you lost will be restored. Even though that loss may be permanent, you feel your anger or resentment will protect you or save you somehow.

Fred wanted to be accepted in the church and worked hard to become a lay pastor. For several years he did well in achieving his goal, until the church leadership changed. Fred ran head on into the new leadership, and they didn't get along. Finally Fred was asked to leave his position as a lay pastor, and he was crushed. He became angry and resentful of everyone. He left the church, embittered, and decided never to return. He began drinking and venting his anger on his family during his drunken rages. He alienated his youngest son and became more bitter as life brought more losses to him.

Years later, when Fred's counselor asked him what he thought his anger had accomplished, Fred replied, "I thought it would protect me from more hurt and rejection, but it actually made me experience more hurt and loss."

You often get stuck in your grief by holding on to emotions that you subconsciously believe will protect you from more pain in your life. This can be helpful for a while, but it becomes harmful if it turns into a pattern.

Often without realizing it, you make decisions that keep you stuck in fear, resentment, guilt, or depression. You may get stuck by making fear your friend to help protect you from failing again. You decide that if you take a risk, you will probably fail, so why try? This keeps you weak and helpless, but at least you feel safe. Or do you? You believe on one level that you gain by holding on to your grief emotions. You get stuck in your anger and resentment and say to yourself, "I can't trust anybody. Everyone lets me down." Rather than face your loss or betrayal, you generalize to a universal betrayal for protection.

You hold on to your sadness or hurts to protect you from more hurts. You may nurse these hurts and injustices to build a stronger wall and then say to yourself, "I'll never be hurt again." However, the wall built of hurts has holes in it, and you can't seem to protect yourself through this sadness. The sadness brings you to the conclusion that nothing is worth living for. That keeps you stuck, keeps you from moving on and contributing again or re-creating. You stay angry at yourself so that you will not make more mistakes, but you find that your punitive decisions do not lessen your sins.

Your decision that it's all your fault doesn't really make it better. It keeps you stuck and prevents you from defining what you want out of life. Because of your guilt, you feel you deserve nothing. So you don't move on to the next stages and recover.

Read the following list of beliefs and check ones that are similar to your thoughts and beliefs right now.

- ☐ "I give up."
- ☐ "I don't care."
- ☐ "God doesn't care."
- ☐ "I'll never love again."
- ☐ "I'll never trust again."
- ☐ "Nothing in life is good."

- ☐ "I'll never be open again."
- ☐ "I'll never be hurt again."
- ☐ "Nothing is worth living for."
- ☐ "I'd be disloyal if I move on."
- ☐ "I can't trust anything or anybody."
- ☐ "It's all my fault. I'm totally to blame."
- ☐ "I'll try harder because I wasn't perfect enough."

Most decisions that keep you stuck are only variations on these themes. Sometimes letting go is forgiving others. Sometimes it's forgiving yourself, and sometimes it's changing your expectations of God. You are the only one who can decide to let go and move forward.

RECOVERY PROBERS

1. In what areas do you find it difficult to stay connected?

2. How do feelings differ from judgments or decisions?

3. Is it difficult for you to tell others how to minister to you in your grief? Why?

4. Are you holding on to guilt and anger toward yourself? How?

5. **What judgments would alienate you from those who could love you?**

6. **How do you feel toward God during this time of grief? What conclusions you are struggling with?**

7. **What unhealthy decisions in your grieving process would keep you stuck?**

RECOVERY GUIDE

Read Hebrews 3:7–9.

1. **How did the Israelites' hardheartedness keep them from receiving God's blessings?**

2. **In what ways are you hardhearted?**

3. **What do you miss out on when your heart is hard?**

Read Hebrews 12:15.

1. **Are you hanging on to an emotion and not receiving the healing you need?**

2. **How does receiving love and grace help you let go of your anger and bitterness?**

Read 1 Corinthians 12:26.

1. **How can you stay connected to other Christians, the body of Christ?**

Read Psalm 42:5.

1. **Is it okay to express your grief emotions to God?**

RECOVERY GOALS

The main goal of this chapter is to point out that you can get stuck in your grief. You can even make your pain linger. You may need to make decisions to help you progress through your grief, like securing a stable environment in which change is at a minimum for a while. If you are depressed, you may need to see a doctor to help you chemically stabilize your depression until you can move on in the grief process. Or you may need counseling to help you face your pain and have the courage to move on.

1. **In what emotion do you get stuck?**

2. **To what unhealthy decision does this lead you?**

3. **Do you feel alienated from yourself? What will you do about it?**

4. **Is there someone you need to forgive? How will you do this?**

5. **Make a commitment to yourself and God to suspend judgment.**

8. A Time of Transition

RECOVERY FOCUS

- Examine the characteristics of the transition stage of grieving.
- Recognize how these characteristics relate to your grief.
- Discover how this transition time is a necessary foundation for your future.

RECOVERY INFORMATION

As you say good-bye to what you lost, you begin to enter an in-between phase, a reflection and questioning time that you need to pass through before you can begin to get on with the rest of your life. Some common characteristics of this transitional phase are *despair, powerlessness, disillusionment, feeling in limbo,* and *review.*

DESPAIR

The transition time can be difficult because you have recognized your loss or change, but you haven't yet begun the process of moving forward with your life. And this leaves you feeling empty. So you are stuck in a state of despair. You will find yourself periodically regressing to the longing and other emotional responses that characterized the saying-good-bye phase. Ultimately, you know that your life can't return to the status quo. Every time you look at this fact, you are left with a desperate sense of despair. There is no going back. Nothing can replace what you have lost. And you feel as if you aren't really going forward.

This sense of despair that the saying-good-bye process leaves you with pushes you to isolate from others. You feel as if no one else can understand your grief. And in many ways this is an accurate perception. Your grief is different from anyone else's. In a sense, a certain amount of disengaging from the world around you is appropriate. Jesus withdrew to the wilderness to pray and fast for forty days when he made the transition into his ministry. A special time away to reflect on the past, consider the present, and plan for the future is very appropriate at this time in the grieving process.

However, don't confuse this with isolating yourself from the support you need. A time of withdrawal needs to be a special time to consider the important questions that arise during this time of transition. It's not a time of lonely isolation to feel sorry for yourself or reject the assistance and support of others.

POWERLESSNESS

Before your loss or change, you felt a certain sense of stability and control over your life. Now you feel as if you have lost control. It seems sometimes that you can do nothing to make a difference. This feeling began early in the grief process and becomes pronounced at this time. You have an overwhelming sense of helplessness. One man said he felt as if he had fallen into a black hole, an inexpressible void that he felt could never be filled. How are you ever going to get along without whomever or whatever you lost? What will you ever do with this emptiness you've felt since your divorce? How will you fill the void that has come since your loved one died?

DISILLUSIONMENT

Disillusionment is often experienced because you believed that your life was going to be more secure than it turned out to be. You felt your marriage would last, your spouse wouldn't die this soon, your job wouldn't end so abruptly, or that you would die before your child. Now you know that your situation will never be the same. Your circumstances have shaken your world view. You have many questions with no answers. And your view of God has also been shaken. You question why you invested so much in your now-broken marriage or why you ever worked so hard for a company that would let you go so easily or why God would take your spouse.

FEELING IN LIMBO

Saying good-bye creates a certain amount of chaos in your life. You feel as if you have said good-bye to a part of you—and you have! The emptiness that comes out of the grieving experience leaves you in limbo. You have moved past your denial to a point where you have said good-bye, but you haven't yet moved significantly forward with a new life.

This can be a scary time because it feels so much like depression. Or it seems that you are moving backward rather than forward. Angelica reached this point in her grief and didn't know where to go. She focused on her immediate problems and became busy with additional activities out of fear of what to do next. Angelica was waiting for something to happen. Eventually she realized that she could begin to make some things happen. She slowed down and rested. Her reflective planning began to turn into some concrete ideas about what she could begin to do with the rest of her life.

This time can also be one of relief and rest. You feel more at ease; some of the demands on your life seem less intense. You can relax and have some fun. Gene retired after twenty-three years with the same company. After a period of grieving the loss of his job, he experienced this limbo period of relief. He didn't want to commit to anything new just yet. He wanted to take in this moment of doing nothing.

After four years of suffering from Alzheimer's disease, Terri's husband died. She mourned his death and missed him greatly. But she also was now able to enjoy her life a little. And before she got on with her life, she wanted to sit and relax. The taxing demands placed on her by her husband's disease seemed unending. But now it was over. She felt she had been given a turn at enjoying retirement.

REVIEW

Out of the emptiness and disillusionment comes a time of review, a time in which you try to make some meaningful sense out of the loss or change. You go over the events of your life and relate them to your loss or change. This helps you better understand your loss or change as well as better navigate a way through your grief. This time of review also helps you create a new life perspective that sets the foundation for you to move forward.

Richard tried to figure out what happened to his marriage by reviewing his family tree. He began to remember what it was like growing up in a home with conflict and a father who drank heavily. As Richard reflected on his growing-up experience, his dating behavior in late high school, his early jobs and how they related to his courtship and subsequent marriage to Nancy, he began to see a pattern. This put his divorce in a more meaningful context, one that helped him push through his disillusionment.

Jennifer quit going to church six months after her young son died.

Her husband wasn't a church-goer, and she stayed home with him on Sunday mornings. Her son's death brought a disillusionment with God and the church. She was mad at God for the way her family life had failed. A husband who was ambivalent about God and a dead child—what kind of Christian life was that? Two years after the death of her child, however, she began reviewing her life in response to her high school reunion. Through this review process, she began to talk with God again. Slowly she repaired her relationship with God and found a new church. Her husband had a much more difficult time with his grief and continued to stay away from church.

Healthy grieving is recognizing your losses or changes and realizing that you can never go back to the way it was. You need to say good-bye to many of your old dreams and goals as well. You then can begin to reflect on new dreams and goals. You can begin to consider new relationships and new opportunities.

Engage in practical activity during this transition phase to help you look toward the future. Read books about grief to become better informed. You can learn how to fix the toilet (if your spouse usually did this) or how to cook or balance the checkbook. You can engage in Bible study and prayer in a new way to discover God's will for your new life.

Julia realized at this point in her grief work that she needed to attend to many tasks she had put off. She had kept her son's bedroom the same since his tragic accident. Now she knew she had to pack his things and turn the room into something useful, like a den.

Robert's fiancée had broken off their engagement when he had moved. For ten months he had not unpacked his boxes from the move. He unpacked only what he needed for day-to-day survival. He finally realized that putting off the unpacking process had only made his grieving more difficult. It was time to unpack and begin a new life in his apartment.

When Rebecca's daughter Lisa married and moved out of the house, Rebecca had shut Lisa's bedroom door. That was over a year ago. Nothing in it had changed. Now Rebecca knew she needed to do something with it. She packed away years of memories and converted the bedroom into a sewing room.

This transition time is a necessary foundation for your future. After a time of saying good-bye, you will need this time to clarify the meaning of your loss, to put it into the context of your larger life, and to rest before you engage yourself in the business of getting on with your life. Through this time you gain perspective on a new direction that your life can take. You will confront and clarify your values and opportunities.

RECOVERY PROBERS

1. How has despair manifested itself in your grieving?

2. What kinds of questions have you asked to express your powerlessness?

3. What kinds of questions have you asked to express your disillusionment?

4. How have you felt your life is in limbo or on hold? What have you done during this time?

5. What have you learned about your life in general and your grief in particular from reviewing your life?

6. What tasks that you have put off now need to get done in order for you to move on with your life?

RECOVERY GUIDE

Read Matthew 4:1–11.

1. When Jesus was about to undertake a new direction in his life, the start of his earthly ministry, he spent forty days and nights in the wilderness. How did this time of transition solidify the meaning of his soon-to-begin ministry?

2. What have you been reflecting on during your time of transition?

3. What has God called you to do?

4. What choices are confusing you or pushing you away from your life's purpose?

Read Galatians 1:13–18.

1. **After the apostle Paul converted to Christianity, he spent a three-year transition time alone in the desert. What things might Paul have learned during his transition as he reflected on his life mission and the Old Testament?**

2. **How did this substantial transition time prepare Paul for ministry?**

3. **What things do you think you need to learn about your Christian life during your time of transition?**

4. **What things do you believe need to be clarified for you before you move on?**

RECOVERY GOALS

This chapter's goal is to help you understand the necessity of a transition period in your grieving before saying hello to a new life.

1. **Have you yet experienced this transition period? If so, have you given yourself permission to relax?**

2. What do you need to accomplish during your transition time?

3. How will you go about doing that?

4. What would happen if you got stuck in this transition time?

5. How will you know you are ready to move on with your life?

9. New Definitions

RECOVERY FOCUS

- Redefine your perspectives and values.
- Define your opportunities and resources.
- Make new connections and new starts.

RECOVERY INFORMATION

Once you've come through the grief stages described in the earlier chapters of this book, your life will begin to take on new definition. Sarah was in a transition because her children were all moving out of childhood. She feeling the loss of the importance of being a mother. Her three children had reached adolescence, the age of "Mom isn't so cool." Sarah also discovered, as she was coming to terms with this loss, that she must have a hysterectomy. This finalized her loss and intensified her grief.

After several months of both physical and emotional recovery, Sarah began to see a new direction in her life. She had been a drama teacher before having children and had a heart to teach again. She decided to explore the opportunities in her field. She found a part-time position at a local high school. She felt alive again and excited to have the opportunity to contribute to the well-being of young people. She began to take the necessary courses to teach again.

NEW PERSPECTIVES

Losses and transitions change your views of life. What seemed important before may no longer seem important to you. Alfonso, in a recovery group, said, "I seem to lose perspective on how important my family is through the urgency of my work. Then I face a loss like my mother's death, and I realize work isn't important at all, but my family is."

Tina said, "I used to be afraid of not being able to handle difficulty in life and was very cautious. Then I lost three family members through car accidents, went through a divorce, moved across the country, got cancer, had several surgeries, and survived. Life doesn't scare me anymore. I'm a survivor."

Dennis said, "I used to focus on pleasing everyone else and doing what I should, but I overlooked my needs until I had a heart attack. I need to take better care of myself. I'm important too."

Loss and change can also radically change your values. The family man who focuses on success and the accumulation of wealth may change his whole orientation when his daughter gets heavily involved in drugs and is disabled in a car accident. The time of reflection that comes after the loss is a time of reevaluation.

Maybe what you believed before is now irrelevant, and your values have to change. You now can't live with the old beliefs without experiencing tremendous incongruence. This forces you to redefine your life and be both a philosopher and theologian, coming up with a world view that will work for you. You may turn inward for the first time in your life, or you may turn to God and find him for the first time. This is a part of the inner journey of the grief process. You ask yourself questions: What is life all about? Who am I? Why am I here? What is my purpose in life or mission? What things are real and which are just illusions? Is what I have been told to believe true? What is worth the risk? Out of the answers to these questions come the definitions that prepare you to move on.

George was fifty-three when he lost his wife to cancer. He felt so alone. His three children had grown and left home before his wife died. Now he felt lost and unattached.

George had spent his life taking care of people. When his father died when George was ten, his mother and three siblings had little financial support. George took over and became the father for his younger brothers and sisters. George worked hard and became very successful in his adult life. He became the head of a successful firm.

After his wife died, it no longer made sense to George to push himself so hard at work. He asked himself the question he had never had the luxury to ask when other people had depended on him for support and care: What do I want to do with my life?

George was disoriented at first, but then he began to reevaluate his life. As a Christian, George knew he wanted to serve, but he also wanted to relax and enjoy life more. He decided to take an early retirement and then went to work in a community organization that helped people who had debt problems. He eventually started dating and married a fun-loving woman, with whom he traveled. His children said, "Dad has sure changed."

NEW LIFE

Just as winter turns to spring, your time of grief will turn into a new life. Many of life's transitions come from moving through the times or stages of life. Childhood ends with a new season of adolescence, and adolescence ends with adulthood.

Adulthood has many seasons or stages as well: establishing a relationship with a spouse, starting a family, developing a career, being promoted in your career or going out on your own, saying good-bye to the children and watching them leave the nest, retiring, and living into old age. Each transition takes its toll on you, and you experience some aspects of grief as you make the transition. Each change involves saying good-bye and saying hello.

Children say good-bye to dependence on their families and say hello to becoming independent and starting their own families. Parents say good-bye to the responsibilities of parenthood as their children leave and say hello to preparing for their own retirement and role as grandparents.

All of these transitions are characterized by an *identification,* a *dis-identification,* and a *new identification.* Perhaps this progression is best understood by looking at the conversion process. When you believe in Christ, the old is put off as the new is put on, as the Scripture says. You identify that your old life is incomplete, sinful. You dis-identify—put off—that old life, and put on the new life, a new identification with Christ as you learn and define who you are in your new relationship with Christ.

You lose your old frame of reference but discover and learn a new frame of reference. You lose hope but develop a new hope. You lose old security and benefits but take risks and establish new securities and benefits. You learn to accept the awkwardness and uncomfortable feelings that go with connecting with something new. A new life comes out of these natural progressions, but not without a cost.

Karl had been flying for the Air Force for a number of years. He had a lot of security and status as a hot dog pilot. He wasn't afraid of anything. However, Karl's life radically changed. He decided to leave the Air Force and become a commercial pilot. He planned this career transition—but not the consequences that came with it. When Karl resigned, he took a large cut in pay to start work for the airlines. The cut in pay upset his marital relationship and caused his family to make some sacrifices. This troubled Karl and made him feel as if he had made a wrong decision to leave the security of the service. He resigned his job with the airlines and went back to work in the reserves. But he began having panic attacks that so overwhelmed him, he felt he could never fly again.

Karl felt stuck in a no-win situation and felt helpless to make any decision that wouldn't increase his pain and discomfort. Karl went to get counseling to help him face his changes and to bring some stability to his transition. His family was brought into the process to help spread the anxiety out and have everyone accept the price of making this change. Karl had always been the hero, the responsible one, and hadn't needed others' help, but now he was willing to accept help. His family responded well and came up with a plan to have Karl return to being a commercial pilot, but in this plan everyone would eventually gain from the initial losses. This helped bring the cost of the transition down to something that was easier to live with, and the whole family began to look forward to the new life in a different city and having Dad as a pilot for the airlines.

RECOVERY PROBERS

1. **What perspectives have changed through your change and loss? How do you see life differently now?**

2. **What beliefs or perspectives are you reevaluating now?**

3. **How have your values changed? What important value has emerged or been clarified through this time of reflection?**

4. **What has become better defined about you? What strengths and weaknesses are more well-defined?**

5. What do you have to give or contribute to others?

6. In what ways do you need to trust more fully in the Lord Jesus Christ?

7. What opportunities are you looking at and which ones are you ignoring?

8. What is your basic mission in life now?

9. What new stage are you entering? What does this stage require of you?

10. Have you begun to see what God has in store for you in the near future? What is it?

RECOVERY GUIDE

Read Acts 1:6–8.

Christ's disciples expected him to be the Messiah king who would deliver Israel from Roman oppression. When Jesus was crucified, many of the disciples lost hope, and some went back to their old jobs. This time of transition forced them to redefine their expectations of God, themselves, and what life was to be for them.

1. **How did Jesus change his disciples' expectations through his death?**

2. **What was the change in their expectations of themselves through this experience?**

God had agreements or covenants with his people down through history. These covenants would change or be redefined as time went on in his relationship with his people. Abraham had a covenant with God. The covenant Isaac and Jacob had with God was based on God's covenant with Abraham. God redefined that Old Covenant and through Jesus Christ brought in a New Covenant.

Read Galatians 3:23–26.

1. **How does the new arise out of the old in this passage?**

2. **How are you to dis-identify with the law in order to identify with Christ?**

RECOVERY GOALS

The goal of this chapter is to help you see how your new definitions will arise as you move into the next stage of recovery from grief.

1. **With what do you need to dis-identify?**

2. **With what do you need to identify in order to solidify the new definition in your life?**

3. **What makes you afraid of the cost of this new identification (discomfort, deferring of rewards, taking risks, etc.)?**

4. **Make a commitment to take calculated risks in moving forward.**

10. Saying Hello

RECOVERY FOCUS

- Rebuild a new life.
- See God's redemption.
- Take a risk.

RECOVERY INFORMATION

In this final stage of recovery, you begin to reengage in life. You take those new definitions, express them, and work from them to re-create a new life. You are able to see opportunities to express yourself in new ways.

This stage is full of risks. You will experience many setbacks and false starts that can be discouraging. It's very easy to become too dependent on results, get discouraged, and lose desire and creativity when results don't occur the way you expect them to.

This process of reconstructing a new life comes from owning your values, dreams, and desires. That inner journey of discovering what is meaningful and real also gives you more independence and autonomy. You have become less dependent on your circumstances and the approval of others. You have a clearer sense of who you are. You aren't as likely to move back to an old security blanket. You are gaining spiritual insights that give you a perspective on how God has been at work. The pieces are coming together. Life makes some sense again. Order is being reestablished. Some of it seems to come together almost magically as if by divine plan.

TIE UP LOOSE ENDS

God is a God of redemption. The Old Testament picture of redemption was that of paying the price to redeem—buy back—a slave who had been in bondage. Redemption brings freedom.

Your grief may be holding you in an emotional bondage, an emotional paralysis. God is committed to redeeming you from bondage, to giving you freedom. The God of redemption restores what is lost; he brings good things out of bad situations; he brings order out of chaos.

In the Old Testament, for example, Joseph was able to look back over his life and see how the difficult experiences of his life played an important part in his development. His difficulties brought him to a place where he could say to his brothers, who had rejected him and cast him away to Egypt, "You intended to harm me, but God intended it for good to accomplish what is now being done, the saving of many lives" (Gen. 50:20). The crucible of Joseph's suffering made him great.

As you have been involved in working through your grief, you have seen that pain often leads to deepened understanding and growth. In the book *Death: The Final Stage of Growth,* Elisabeth Kubler-Ross and Roy and Jane Nichols reiterate this truth: "The ultimate goal of grief work is to be able to remember without emotional pain and to be able to reinvest emotional surpluses. While the experience of grief work is difficult, slow, and wearing, it is also enriching and fulfilling. The most beautiful people we have known are those who have known defeat, known suffering, known struggle, known loss, have found their way out of the depths. These persons have an appreciation, a sensitivity, and an understanding of life that fills them with compassion, gentleness, and a deep loving concern. Beautiful people do not just happen."

One of the loose ends that gets tied up in this stage is reconciling relationships that were broken during times of loss and change. During your grief process, you may have tried to protect yourself from more hurt by distancing yourself from certain people. You may have been angry and bitter with some people. Trust has been broken, leaving you feeling lost and helpless.

During this final stage of grief, you may be ready to forgive and even reconcile if it is possible. You may finally feel free to be honest with your thoughts, feelings, and desires. The inner journey brings clarity out of confusion, and as you see yourself more clearly, you may see your relationships in a more compassionate and forgiving way.

When Paul's mother died, he felt his sister, Anne, wasn't there to help support him or his dad. Even though Anne knew her mother had been very sick, she didn't fly in until the day before the funeral. Paul felt he had to carry the load by himself. He didn't say anything to his sister, but he resented her deeply. He didn't want to start a scene that would upset his father further. Paul's loss of his mother came on the heels of a job change for him. This combination of change and loss put Paul in a depression for several months.

As Paul began to come out of his grief and depression, he realized his alienation from his sister. He wrote her a letter and explained how he had been angry and resentful toward her. He said he wanted to clear up this obstacle in their relationship. Anne responded favorably, and they had a long talk the next time she came to town. That brought reconciliation. Anne apologized for not being there. She explained her situation and her fears of seeing her mother die. They cried together over the loss of their mother. They said they didn't want to lose each other.

Paul felt that part of being able to move on was to heal this relationship. He had the energy to do this as he recovered from his grief. With his conscience now clear, Paul had more energy to apply to rebuilding his life.

TAKE A RISK

Just as a flower can't spring up in midwinter from frozen ground, even if it had the desire to, you won't be able to grow and rebuild until the timing and conditions are right. *Opportunity, resources, desire, action,* and *risk* all play a part in the rebuilding stage.

Are you ready to step forward and act? Have you developed the competency, or are you willing to develop it? If the door opens, will you walk through it? Are you willing to pay the price? Often that price involves paying dues again in your life: humbling yourself, learning anew, and being the student instead of the master. Stepping forward may seem like stepping backward when you are rebuilding because of where you have been.

Joe had a very successful business that paid him a large salary. After the recession, his business collapsed, leaving him without a job. He stayed in limbo for a long time, looking for a job with a comparable salary. After months of looking, Joe realized he would have to take a position at a much lower salary. He found a job with advancement opportunities that would allow him to express his heart's desires in creative ways. Joe had more freedom in this position, giving him great rewards.

Desire plays a large part in the rebuilding process. Desire will help you push beyond dead-end experiences to find another starting place. Desire is an important component of Christian faith. The great men and women of faith were people who demonstrated a desire for God. They desired things they couldn't yet see and were confident in seeking after them. Hebrews 11:6 says, "And without faith it is impossible to please God, because anyone who comes to him must believe that he exists and that he rewards those who earnestly seek him." These heroes of the faith followed God because they expected him to come through, but they also desired to please God by walking in faith. Faith is the opposite of fear and moves you to trust God and take risks.

Many great people have suffered tremendous losses in their lives. But they chose to work through their grief, take risks, and rebuild their lives. Wilma Rudolf had polio as a child and fought back to become one of the greatest female track stars in this century, winning three gold medals in the 1960 Olympics. Abraham Lincoln ran for office without succeeding several times, and two of his children died. These, among other failures and losses, led him into deep depression. Out of his losses he became one of our greatest presidents. William Durant lost everything he had several times in his life and came back to create one of the largest companies in American industry, General Motors.

RECOVERY PROBERS

1. What is the most difficult aspect of rebuilding your life?

2. With whom do you need to reconcile to be able to move forward?

3. How do you see the broken pieces of your life fitting together?

4. What fears about rebuilding bother you at this point?

5. How can you hinder the process of rebuilding by focusing on results?

RECOVERY GUIDE

Read Psalm 30:11–12.

1. How has the psalmist's life been set free, redeemed?

2. How are you beginning to feel free from the emotions that held you in bondage while you were deep in grief?

3. How is God redeeming your difficult experiences?

Read 2 Corinthians 5:18–19.

1. God is committed to reconciling broken relationships. How did he reconcile the world to himself?

2. Do you have relationships that have reconciled as you have moved through your grief? Which ones? What changed to bring reconciliation?

3. What relationships still need to be reconciled?

4. What connections need to be reestablished?

Read Revelation 21:1–4.

1. What is the promise of this new creation?

2. How does this give you hope?

RECOVERY GOALS

The goal of this chapter is to show how rebuilding is the final stage of the recovery process. This stage happens when your emotional energy is free from the pain of loss and can be invested creatively to reconstruct and reconnect your life. You may not be in this stage yet, but it will come. There is risk required on your part to say hello again and to move forward.

1. What risks do you need to be prepared to make before you can move forward?

2. What signs of rebuilding do you see in your life?

LEADER'S GUIDE

WORKING WITH PEOPLE WHO HAVE EXPERIENCED LOSS AND CHANGE

Leaders of this group must be comfortable with intense emotions and facilitate their expression. There can be no "Don't feel that way," or "I'll fix you" allowed in the group. Because it is often scary for people to face their emotions, any hindrance may cause them to pull back and not do their grieving. Grieving people have lots of their own feelings to work through. They also have many difficult questions, and it is important, as part of the grief process, that they struggle through them to their own answers. Leaders, then, should respect people's emotions, resist giving pat answers, and trust that God works through pain to bring healing and new growth.

PURPOSE OF GROUP

Involve the group in defining this purpose so that they have some personal ownership in the group dynamic and can define some of their personal goals.

1. To provide people with the hope of recovery
2. To give information about grief and loss
3. To provide a safe environment where people can grieve
4. To help those who grieve to heal and grow
5. To point those who grieve to God for help

GROUP FORMAT

Suggested size of group: 8–12 members.

Suggested length of time for the group: 12–15 weeks, spending 1–2 hours per session.

Opening Sessions

1. Define the purpose of the group and ask why people are there.
2. Read together the Group Ground Rules, found on the following pages.
3. Ask each person to take 10–15 minutes to give his or her personal background and tell his or her story.
4. Define your expectations of attendance and workbook involvement. Get clear commitments from group members.

5. Establish a support network for the group members. Talk about meeting outside the group for coffee, exchange phone numbers, and the like.

Workbook Sessions

1. Open each session with prayer.
2. Share victories, especially those related to previous chapters.
3. Discuss the various sections of the week's chapter.
4. Share current struggles. Allow people time to work on struggles. Bring tissues and allow time for grieving.
5. Pray together each week.

Closing Sessions

1. Focus on what has been gained by reflecting on victories.
2. Talk about what relationships have been meaningful.
3. Make a commitment to have a reunion in three months.
4. Talk about where people can now find support.

GROUP GROUND RULES

1. All conversations in the group are confidential and may not be shared with anyone outside the group. If permission is asked and everyone is comfortable, an exception can be made. Protection leading to trust building is a goal of this group.
2. These groups aren't open groups, which means that others can't be invited after the group starts. There can be exceptions if the group and the group leader agree.
3. It is important that people share what they are experiencing and that they don't generalize. They need to own their own feelings and not judge others. For example, "Christians don't understand what it is like to lose a loved one," versus "I feel hurt when people at my church make insensitive comments about my loss."
4. Members aren't responsible for other members; group members aren't responsible to give advice, excuse other people's actions, minimize other's feelings, or fix hurting people. What this means is there is no cross-talk allowed. Group members may share experience from their point of view if someone in the group needs that information. Be careful not to minimize or be critical of others' feelings.
5. Listen without interrupting (unless you are the leader and

responsible to watch the time in sharing). Each person's story and experience is valuable. Each group member is valuable.

6. Avoid using "shoulds" or "oughts" in the group, either for yourself or others.
7. If a group member becomes anxious about the group experience, talk about it in the group. If a group member wants to quit the group over fearful feelings or resentment, talk about it in the group. Do a reality check with the person, helping him or her to see if the fear is warranted or just a part of the recovery process. Honesty is a key to successful recovery. And honesty can be practiced at times like this in the group.
8. Stay on the goals and purposes of the group and keep conversations directed.
9. Make and express additional ground rules that would make this group a more effective place in which recovery can occur.

GROUP PROCESS

Groups form in stages. The initial stage is one of bonding, a stage in which group members share about themselves and find out if the group is safe. The leader's role is to facilitate safety and openness. Leaders need to work toward giving everyone the opportunity to share. Be careful not to allow group members to rescue each other.

In later stages, the group members will jockey for positions. Don't be surprised if group members challenge your leadership. Your role is to avoid thinking like a rescuer or a victim and to move the group and its members toward personal responsibility, godliness, and healthy thinking. This gives opportunity for real dialogue between group members and for teaching of new skills.

In the last stages, the group members need to learn to let go and say good-bye in a healthy way. Help group members to focus on what they have learned and how they have grown. Help group members reflect on their victories and express their joy from relationships. Your role will be one of helping members not to rationalize but to face their feelings of loss and to express tenderness to each other.

REFERRALS

People in grief often experience depression, overwhelming feelings, and high levels of anxiety. Any signs of deep depression such as insomnia, significant weight loss or weight gain, withdrawal from life tasks, or suicidal thoughts must be referred to a pastor, counseling professional, or hospital. Other issues may arise that would call for referrals. When developing a referral list, consider:

1. Caring churches that minister to people
2. Treatment centers
3. Christian counselors
4. Social service agencies

SUGGESTED QUALIFICATIONS FOR GROUP LEADERS

For maximum effectiveness, leaders will have

1. experienced grief and have worked through some of their own issues in relationship to this grief.
2. been a Christian for several years and have a basic knowledge of the Bible.
3. a dynamic relationship with Christ and a commitment to pray daily for their group members.
4. experience facilitating a group. If possible, leaders will first serve as co-leaders of a group before having primary leadership responsibilities.
5. experience teaching and practicing basic communication skills, like "using 'I messages,'" "reflective listening," "problem ownership," "request making," and the like.
6. accountability to the leaders of the facility in which the support group meets.
7. wisdom on knowing when to refer group members for professional help.
8. Christ-centered motives for leading a group.
9. no anxiety about strong expressions of emotion.

SUGGESTED READINGS

Bayly, Joseph. *The View from a Hearse.* Elgin, Ill.: David C. Cook, 1969.

Bridges, William. *Transitions: Making Sense of Life's Changes.* Reading, Ma.: Addison-Wesley, 1980.

Convissor, Kate. *Young Widow.* Grand Rapids: Zondervan, 1992.

Deits, Bob. *Life After Loss: A Personal Guide Dealing with Death, Divorce, Job Change and Relocation.* Tucson, Arizona: Fisher Books, 1988.

Lewis, C. S. *A Grief Observed.* San Francisco: Harper & Row, 1961.

Vesberg, Branger E. *Good Grief.* Philadelphia: Fortress, 1989.

Vetter, Robert J. *Beyond the Exit Door.* Elgin, Ill.: David C. Cook, 1974.